Just Enough For The City

poems by

Jo'rell H. Whitfield

w4ml
writing4mylife

Cover art by Jo'rell H. Whitfield

Copyright © 2018 Jo'rell H. Whitfield

All rights reserved.

ISBN-13: 9781790675678

GRATITUDE

I give gratitude to the creator of all things. I am grateful for the gifts I've been given, and the beautiful souls that have helped me bring them to light. I am grateful to the people of all these cities I've been to, who have taken me in like family, showing me unique city perspectives I would not know otherwise. I am grateful for '80's New York that birthed & raised me. Thank you to Queens! You will always be home. Thank you to friends & family... you all know who you are. Thank you to every fan in every country. Thank you Des for BUILDING with me. LOVE. ALWAYS

TABLE OF CONTENTS

1. J.E.F.T.C — pg. 1
2. No Love in the ♡ of the City — pg. 3
3. Baltimore — pg. 7
4. SportsCenter — pg. 11
5. In Chicago — pg. 15
6. Older — pg. 19
7. Lenox & 119th — pg. 25
8. Gentrification — pg. 29
9. Crooked — pg. 33
10. To Tamir — pg. 39
11. Say Her Name — pg. 43
12. Sports Center (Fight Night) — pg. 47
13. Fried Rice — pg. 51
14. E Train to 34th — pg. 55
15. Times Square — pg. 59
16. City Love — pg. 63

Just Enough For The City

Just
Cling to
Whatever
Light might shine bright
Enough through the dark
That shrouds this naked town
Wrapped only in silks of sin
To unravel what keeps one bound
One must drown in the sounds from within
Or be drowned out within the city's sounds
For here is where the journey begins
And ends the same, in pain or kind
The only way to survive
And make it out alive
Is to find yourself
Then learn to love
And let the
City
Die

One

TWO

No Love in the ♥ of the City

This city doesn't love you.
It was made from survival
It exists without you here...
It wasn't waiting for your arrival
Its ego rivals yours
Though it knows it's meant to be here
While you're still not even sure.
This city will not mourn you...
This city will endure.
It will not ~~abate~~ or cave
Under the pressures of oppression
It is one with the obsession
It was created by slaves
Waves and WAVES OF SLAVES

This city can't love you,
It wasn't made that way
It was built on freedom
It never stayed that way

THREE

It might have been etched in cobble stones
That have long since been paved away unceremoniously,
Without a poem to pen
This city doesn't loan or lend...
You gotta pay to play.
Whether native or foreign
You gotta pay to come,
And pay to stay.
It doesn't care where you're from
Or to whom you pray
There is only the god of light
At the end of the day.
No matter what borough you burry into
The city still sees you as prey
In the mile-high mountains
Or concrete jungles
By the gulf, or the coast,
Or the beach or the bay
You will worm your way
Through this life
If you want to live under these lights
Over-exposed to all this plight

Four

You will learn to sway
FAR LEFT OR FAR RIGHT
Debate over the WRONGS
March for all the RIGHTS
You will clash in opposition
Despite
How much you are ALL ALIKE
Imbued in the same illusion
A beast of the same Hype
You will scale the walls of the same confusion,
Just to fall from the same Heights
And THIS city will LET you.
You will climb AND REPEAT...
AND THIS CITY WON'T CATCH you.
You will seek to be made whole
Through the pains of plain truth
Just to claim a piece of the city...
THAT will NEVER CLAIM you!

Five

Six

Baltimore

Beat up lil seagull
On a marble stair
Trying to find the ocean
Looking everywhere
Hard times in the city
In a hard town by the sea,
Not quite Cali days...
But if you seek...
You can find the sun peek
Through an alleyway
There is art in the darkness
Barrels of crabs
Pinching each other's shells
Nipping at each other's tails
In the dark pits.
Feathers tip the scale of the heartless
Teenagers follow lieutenants and sergeants.
Seven

IN BOLD DAY
NEW HOPPERS LEARN OLD WAYS
THAT GET BAKED IN, DEEP FRIED
AND SPRINKLED WITH OLD BAY
THE thirst WASHED DOWN WITH TEA
& LEMONADE
NEW BUILDINGS BUILT ON TOP OF
PEOPLE IN THE WAY
THEY
Compliment the CORNERS WITH Chipotles
AND COLD STONES
LIFE IS AS COLD AS Rita's Snow Cones
OLD HATE BURIED UNDER RENOVATED
ROW HOMES
BALTIMORE :
Once ROAMED BY SURVIVORS OF
GENOCIDE
STARVED & Kept Alive ...
Just to Be GENTRIFIED
Separated AND MISPLACED AND Left
~~A CRAB CAKE FROM Phillip's~~ IN
ONA' EAST | DESPAIR
ONA' WEST

eIGHT

Black seagulls on marble stairs
Under heat
Over-stressed
Over-watched by police
On the run from undercovers
Trying to discover some peace
Under blue lights
Pawns that never learn to move
Right
In conflict with pieces that choose life
The board so black & white
The Queens are sometimes Queer
The Queer are sometimes Queens
The Kings are Dope Boys
And sometimes inbetween
The Castle is Church
 But some Bishops are thieves
If you Believe
Then the game is never what it seems
A roar from the stadium
Can't drown out the screams
Of the city,
 Its moans!
Nine

Junkies bop down Fayette
Shaking in old bones
Clutching Natty Boh's
Afros, locs, twists, & French pleats
Stomachs lined with chicken boxes
and Pit Beef
and Lake Trout
Daily bread from fast food,
liquor stores and take out
While developers and investors
Meet at the Steakhouse
Debates and handshakes
Over steaks, crabs & whiskey
Shared ~~plans~~ smiles
Over plans to
Take back the city.
With little resistance or revolt
A politician chokes
    From a laugh and cigar smoke
All smoke and mirrors
A city screams her pains
...but no one is there to hear her.

Ten

SportsCenter

SportsCenter the center of my HOME
Around a couch 8 men pretend to be grown
Debating wordly topics like:
Early pick for M.V.P.
"This the last year for Golden State and KD."
"Lebron ain't never gonna get another ring..."
Pause for a second.
The door bell rings —
Whole room stops.
Peek out the window,
Make sure it ain't the cops...
"Nah, that's my nigga June from up the block...! He good"
And then it's right back to the crops, the herb

eleven

Break it down, twist it up,
Pass it right to Pops
Pops passes to Moms
Moms pass it to.... Grandma
Auntie in the corner sippin Hennessey
No Grand Mar...
None of that soft shit!
We drinking & smoking around 4 kids
Leaking poisons into their lungs
Like faucets
But this is life, and we floss it.
Nothing in our closets.
We are who we are.
Plus, the kids know what it is
They know the difference between
Grown folks business
(Put 'em in the room with the video
game... they'll mind their business)
A sister comes in
Tells the 8 that a young one got
Suspended....
Twelve

The ~~scene~~ shifts and bends
as ~~&~~ pretenders
jump in the role of men
lending the young one lessons
in deference
Swollen jaws and soft behinds
the reference,
~~But the love is in the message~~
Takes a village to raise a young one,
and the young one gets the message
. . .
Then it's back to the Jets
or the Mets
or the Knicks
or the Lakers
All we talk about
is sports, bitches, and paper!
And ~~pop~~ shit.
The girls call it gossip
We call it Block shit...

Thirteen

Who got shot,
And how the feds is watching
Who got laid down,
And who got locked in
* Another Sports Debate *
Better point guard:
   J. Kidd or Stockton

* Another Blunt circles the Room *
The smoke has us boxed in
With the aroma from the oven...
The kitchen is Rockin'!
Tin Foil <u>EVERYWHERE</u>

Chicken in the pots and the pans
Bake the Mac & the cheese, and
The yams, and the peas and the ham
And it feeds all the fam.
You embraced now... we all fam,
Grab a plate... eat what you can.
No need for grace... The Lord
          Already blessed
Fourteen   The Hands

IN CHICAGO

in Chicago, right now,
fourteen 14-year-olds are
preparing to air-it-out.
The plan was always to exterminate
but now it seems
they've got the means
to really carry it out
Extreme
are the measures they've gone to
to pawn youth
off.
My nigga told me they found a
bunch of guns in the back of a
U-Haul
left unattended
parked right in the middle of the
ghetto YOU ALL live in...
Fifteen

So no matter How you feel ABOUT THE WAR
You   ALL   IN   IT!
IN OAKLAND
THEY CALL IT "BABY BAGHDAD"
INSTEAD OF "BABY KEMET"
WHY IS THIS?
IS IT BAD Police WORK,
OR GREAT GUN BUSINESS?
IS IT THE ENVIORNMENT
Responsible FOR RAISING Violets up
IN violence?
OR is it THE pitching of "NO SNITCHING"
THAT LEAVES US ALL out Here Silent?
IS it the Science?
THAT Keeps A TEEN Huddled over
A STOVE WITH PYREX?
"~~Nothing to loose could ever~~
~~Yefelds.~~"

Sixteen

Life After Death Booming From
  Boom Box
"Nothing To Loose"
     Tatoo'D over eyelids.
I Wish a Nigga Would!
Reads on the screens of his iris
What He Sees Through The Trees
is a Compton on Fire
A Philly Damaged And Fatigued
A Baltimore Worse Than ISIS
A Camden Starved And Famished
A Michigan in Midst of Crisis
An Entire State That Won't Fix The Water..

But will still Root For The Tigers
                    + Lions
                    + Bears.
       Oh, My!

Seventeen

eighteen

OLDER

I'm older now..... wiser
Used to keep weed in my Trapper-Keeper divider
I thought it was a safe place
Used to keep my ID in my wallet while driving,
Now,
I keep that bitch up in the visor,
You know.... just in case.
See, I used to not trust the police
Now,
I trust them to be exactly who they say they are...
Wayward
I'm older now,
I know that "Hey Cuz"
In certain neighborhoods means
Nineteen

You better be with the Shits
Or with a shit-load of Bloods
(or Crypts)
Speaking of blood...
Yours better not be filled with shit.
You know,
    Calories + Carcinogens
You better learn how to cleanse!
You better <u>NOT</u> go without
Knowing that all comes from within
Speaking of within...
You better go there more often
You better lay there, stay there,
Pray there more often.
I'm older now,
More often I use more caution
I used to idolize the hustlers
Now I see what hustling's cost
    them...

TWENTY

Custom Bullet-Holes
 For jewelry that's costume.
I used to drink + drive while high,
Not certain if I'd die soon
For some, when it rains, it pours,
For me, when it rained, it Typhoon'd

Hopeless
Like a baby being made from tied tubes
The pressure was higher than Diabetes
Type 2

I was raised to believe
in the disease of white truth
But I'm older now,
And know it can all be eased with
the right food!
 Speaking of food...

TWENTY-ONE

You know we eat DEAD meat?
Baste it, bake it, fry it way
down deep.
Eat two patties and fake fries,
Then lay down to a sound sleep
Not judging anybody
I'm just saying what we think.
I'm older now, and know how
the body processes a quarter-
                    pounder
After-hours, after hours of
pounding down watered-down
drinks. Speaking of Drinks...

You know we need water, right?
Gallons of the shit, not kinda-sorta
like
And I know we all going within,

TWENTY-TWO

And melanin is in
But it's not meant for you to hoard the light.
I'm older now,
What used to hold me down
I now used to move towards the light
I now own my moments
Sight beyond sight
My sword swing through all omens
Moroccan Egyptian from Queens
That read through all Romans...
In King's English.
Also fluent in hood shit, which means
I can articulate the anguish
And trauma... word to my momma,
And hers, and hers, and hers, and yours.
And every woman who has endured
Nurturing in love & peace
While always on the verge of war
I hear & know like never before!
Twenty-three

TWENTY-FOUR

Lenox & 119th

Maybe my wayward memories
Render me
Helpless victim of nostalgia,
But I can't help but wonder...
What happened to Harlem?
As I stare out a bistro window
Lenox Ave exists as some wounded widow
Once married to heroes like
Claude and Hughes and
Duke and Baldwin
And Bessie and Gertrude and
Augusta and Zora.
At a time when Negroes
Were slain & slaughtered
There were Blacks on Lenox with
Minks and ~~Fedoras~~

Twenty-Five

And Dresses and Suits and
   Buicks and Fords
Beautiful Black Men on
Beautiful Black Accord with
Beautiful Black Wives Raising
Beautiful Black Daughters
In the Midst of American Chaos
Creating
Beautiful Black Order
Nothing short of
A Renaissance.
I stare out and reminisce over
my plate of penne sauce,
My second dish
I catch a glance with a Homeless
Man,
His eyes remind me of my Decadence
As I sit Here and sip
My espresso Drip
Twenty-Six

And enjoy the brewed flavors
Pull out my Wall St. Journal
And flip through a few pages
I see how I seem like
I'm just like the new neighbors
Moving in on Town Homes and
Brownstones left vaccant
Move in
And push out a community left waiting
For whatever was supposed to be
Trickled Down from Reagan
Waiting - seems synonymous with
this "African-American Nation"
Obvious,
There's nothing like
African-American patience
That keeps us Hoping & praying
For a payout or payment
Twenty-Seven

Patience of a mustard seed growing
From underneath the pavement
So we struggle to pay rent
Single mothers hustle the graveshift
While their sons hug the block
Like they're still chained
To SLAVE SHIPS

A blonde with blue eyes
Enters the shop with swayed hips
Her unwitting smile
Reminds me how
HARLEM is NOW...
WAY Hip!

TWENTY-EIGHT

Gentrification

My mom and I used to go to my
favorite pizza spot after school.
We'd walk there
after hopping off the $1 van
on any random afternoon
It's gone now.
In its space is some place
that sells random macaroons...
and little cupcakes
This all happened so swiftly.
They seem to get things so quickly
while we must wait
They must hate us ... the way
they pass without words to say
without a nod of acknowledgement.
Twenty-Nine

A Hello, or Good Day!
Just a silent patience
   For us to fade away
As if
We appeared from nowhere
As if
We hadn't made a way.
As if
These avenues had been bartered
As if
These boulevards built over us
Weren't named after our martyrs
Marked by the marches
            + sit-ins
Of our mothers and fathers
I can see how some of us
Don't even bother
Rhetoric from politicians
   Fed like fodder
To the neighborhood cattle
Thirty

The hi-rises cast
  an inescapable shadow
that foreshadows things to come
Living in this place
  has always been a battle
And there still ain't **NOWHERE** to run
Not even to Seattle or Asheville
or Dallas or Austin
In **THESE** places and more
Liquor stores turn to Lofts & Condos
Supermarkets Disappear......
                    PRONTO!
From Dade County to Toronto...
No investments to be made
When the Mayor's the Head Honcho,
we,
the **URBAN** people, aren't Relevant
in this **URBAN** Development

Thirty-one

We... just become the elephants
in this rennovated room
standing out like candy shops
on a new block
full of vegan spots
We will be forgot
if we don't innovate soon.

THIRTY-TWO

CROOKED

In the heat of the moment
An officer could lose its cool.
He's stressed from bills
Wishing he was still in school.
His engineering skills
Turn into cheap thrills of pulling
Brown boys over
Giving them deep chills
Pulls over whoever he feels
At will.
At lights... (woop! woop!)
At stop signs (woop! woop!)
He seeks I.
But hides behind shield
Soccer dad on the weekend,
But with a uniform on...

THIRTY-THREE

He's a soldier on the killing field
The corners of my neighborhood
His command post.
He's an extra long day,
And a smart-ass kid away
From going Rambo.
Patrolling those that hate him
A little too much for him to handle
A wife and a newborn;
A handful
His career is an anvil,
An anchor.
A pain; a sore; a canker
Two over-night shifts lead to anger

RAGE

This his 4th year on the force
He's still chasing dope boys half
his age
Huffin' & Puffin'

THIRTY-FOUR

'Cause he's over-weight
So you know he's cuffin'
Anybody over 8...
He loves the law...
It's just the niggas he hates
The dark shades
The gold chains
The "Dread" locks
The box-braids
The white tee's
The black J's
The rims, the Caprices, the Chevorlets
The limo-window tints
The fiends, the Jons
The bimbos, the pimps
The Bloods, the Crypts,
      The Gangs!

It's just....
Not enough trees for us
  To hang from...

Thirty-Five

But there's enough streets for us to <u>BANG</u> on!
Hood shit claims the mind,
There's a war going on,
And the law lays the mines
The Claymores
Rides around town
   with his windows down.
The sweet scent of agony
Smells like Claiborne
Spray on the misery
To him,
  it just compliments the imagery
"Fuck 'em! Let 'em burn!
  Let 'em idolize the industry. Talk
that tough talk on them videos...
But if I catch 'em out here in
  the streets it's...."
WOOP WOOP!! THAT'S THE SOUND OF THE POLICE!

Thirty-six

WOOP! WOOP! THAT'S THE SOUND OF THE BEAST
RED LIGHT, BLUE LIGHT, HANDS UP! FREEZE!
NOW,
IF THE PROJECTS GOT THE ROACHES, THAN THE REST OF US ARE FLEAS ON THE BIG DOG OF THE LAW. THEY'VE GOT A GRIP OF FEAR ON THE PEOPLE, PIT-BULL-JAW-LOCKED, GLOC-9 COCKED, NO SAFETY, NO RUNNING FROM THE JAKES, B. NO HIDING FROM THE JAKES, SON, ESPECIALLY THE SNAKE ONES, THE VULTURES, WHO CIRCLE AROUND MY NEIGHBORHOOD PREYING ON THE CULTURE.
RED LIGHT, BLUE LIGHT
PULL OVER LIKE YOU'RE SUPPOSED TO. DON'T BE NO FOOL. CAUSE IN THE HEAT OF THE MOMENT, AN OFFICER COULD LOSE HIS COOL...
THIRTY-SEVEN

Thirty-Eight

To Tamir,

To Tamir,
A few years ago
A few thousand tears ago
You were here
With no worries of being buried
Buried in child-like cares
Free from the fears
Of adults sworn to care
And protect... and serve
The nerve of us to ignore how
The two rarely connect
These events become chains
Engraved in our chest
These links may not enslave
But have the same ~~effect~~
That wave effect, that
~~Hashtag~~ marks the grave effect
~~Thirty-nine~~

A judge drags his feet on the case
citing the family would rather get paid,
than get justice.
I guess
Tamir might as well have been shot with a musket
to show how far we've all regressed
If killing black boys was some sort of horse,
I'm guessing, of course,
it'd be beaten to death!
If I named all the names of the ones we have lost
I'd be labeled a race-hater
or even obsessed.
I guess,
what's taken the hardest
forty

is my color remains the
TARGET

Regardless of what I possess
I possess the right to rights
including the rights to possess
But dont possess the <u>Right to</u>
<u>Life</u>
That still concludes in certain
death... yet...
We still progress.
With Black Lives Mattering on
our Breath
We march on while you rest
in a Peace we'll probably
never see a piece of,
Peace Love.

Forty-one

FORTY-TWO

Say Her Name

How do you go from failure to
signal a lane change
to dead in jail by suicide?
How are you and I
not consumed by the fuel inside?
What is the last thing you say
when you walk out the door
knowing today is the day
they'll come take you away
forever...
For failure to signal a lane change
— nothing seems to —
No matter how we vote,
or who we cling to.
The death in those sirens
still ring true & swallow you
forty-three

You may support the Blue
But what about when they follow you.

TARGET
YOU

Pull you over for no reason
And then proceed to bark @ you
A Black woman. Alone. Driving
By herself.
Hunted down & yanked out her car
By someone who's meant to help.
How do you avoid this drama?
How is this pain not felt
How does that reignite your trauma?
What does that do for Mental Health?
How do you feel when you know
You can't ask for a hand, and
You're being pushed out of the range
Of the dashboard cam
Forty-Four

And you try not to panic
As you hope to survive
But then hope fades to black
When backup arrives
And you're handled and prodded
And teased and trapped
Then you're screaming face-down
With their knees in your back
And you wince out in pain
As two officers restrain
And you yell out:
"ALL THIS FOR A FUCKING
　　　LANE CHANGE?!"
And they drag you to your feet
And bag you in broad day
And with only one witness watching
They drag you away
And you thank that lone witness
For filming these men

Forty-Five

Not knowing that no one
will see you again.
You disappear.... with the law,
in custody, into the fog
Before the belly of the beast,
You are first crushed under its
 paw
You are kidnapped by the clan
and taken away from fam
and what happens the next three
days... no one will ever understand.
How can the world sit in place
with all these questions left to stand?
And the most pertinent left
 unanswered...
Whatever happened to
 SANDRA BLAND?

Forty-six

Sports Center
(Fight Night)

Ayo! The fight's on!!

House full of people...
All the lights on.
60-inch in the corner, we moved
the furniture for this one.
Red cups get filled with whatever
gets poured,
While my main man twists one.
Or two, or three, or four
Ladies just walked through the door.
Already had enough liquor,
But they came in with more
Sun-dresses & weaves the scene,
Hip-Hop is the score
Hood shit might be the theme,
But love is at its core

Forty-Seven

Bunsen Burners heat up the tin foil
That keeps the meat warm
That feeds the carnivores...
The meat-lovers
Cauliflower, Broccoli, + Blue cheese
For the others
A kitchen full of Aunties, Sisters,
And Cousins, and Mothers
Some of them THOTS,
ALL of them LADIES
All of them off-duty from their babies,
So ain't no babying the shots
Grown women being grown
'Cause ain't no babies in the spot.
Just baby-soft Apple-Bottoms.
One brushes up against me to ash
her blunt in a Snapple bottle...
Could tell:
She was made from the best stuff on earth

Forty-Eight

Convincing ourselves we love this
Must be the best bluff on Earth
The reality is inhaled
With my next puff of Earth.
Higher goes the tones and pitches
Of these sisters + mothers
Now calling each other BITCHES!
With Smiles,

And Love and Hugs
And Pictures... and Selfies
(See) The relationship with her Bitch
is the one that's most healthy
in her life.
For most of us here,
The real fight is with life
More than Mayweather, we just
here for the get together,
Forty-Nine

Here for the Sprite ... and O.J.
The mimosas
Let's make the most of this openness
Drink & dance our pains away
Till we're motionless
- 4th Round
Huddled 'round the big screen
Hoping this
Fight might last
      Longer than the last
The longer the rounds,
    The longer it lasts.
The daps, the pounds, the flirting
The laughs....
The feeling.

FIFTY

Fried Rice

Fried Rice & Rib Tips
And Nuggets and Nibblets
And Breasts and Wings and Bisquits
And Fries.
Napkins and Straws
And Spoons and Forks
And Garlic & Salt
On Slices and Pies
Pepperoni and Sausage
Fruit Punch and Orange and Cherry
And Grape and Pineapple Fantas
Distorted Order
Soaked in Quarter-Water Mantras
Little Princes Turn Queens
When the Closets Can't Hold the
Monsters

Fifty-One

Able slings 'caine
at a b-ball game that
Coke sponsors
— Talent for tournament jerseys —
A fair and honest trade
Trophies make for memories
But memories are made to fade
Like jeans... and glory
The war of Spades played
Less for the game,
More for the stories
Mixed in with Reminiscing of
the Golden-Age Knicks and
The Bulls vs. Pistons
And Big-Shot Bob Horry
Mixed in
With a spliff and
A 5th or a shortie

Fifty-Two

Whatever bridges the gap between
happiness and shortly
thereafter
Fears captured
on corners in caption
New neighbors with new faces
Maybe due to inaction
This play is no play,
But remains in action!

FIFTY-THREE

Fifty-Four

E Train to 34th

Sometimes I long for train rides
And who I might meet
In the eyes of a stranger's
Glance of pity
As the E train sways back & forth
Along the veins of the city.
I just might find peace
Here, sub-level
Down next to the Devil
I find myself amongst thousands
of Gods
On their way to different boroughs
To and from odd jobs
Barreling down these underground
Burrows
You can taste the city's peril

Fifty-Five

Wreaking like Rotten Cadavers
Nine to five Bodies Bruised & Battered
Smooth Chocolate Godiva Skin
Mesh with Chinese and Koreans
As if they were Kin
A Man Yawns From Long Days Work
And can nearly taste the Sin
A Woman Swirls Chopsticks in
Shark Fin Soup
An inner-city youth
Draped in SUPREME and NIKE
BOOTS

Stand Shoulder-to-Shoulder with
Dull Business Suits
A Woman Sells mangos, yo-yo's,
And Batteries
A Homeless man Shrouded in
Catastrophe, Speaks to Himself
And Anyone who will Listen
Fifty-Six

A blind man begs for change
when he should beg for vision
This must be the perfect world
Christians envisioned
Down here next to the Devil
is humanity's collision.
A surgical incision along
culture and religion shows
our inevitable division
that only a train ride can provide
Automatic doors slide open & close
the entire event is poetry in prose
I can't help but wonder
where everyone goes
when they leave this underground
lair,
and disappear up the concrete
stairs...
And into
         Concrete Jungle.
Fifty-Seven

Fifty-eight

Times Square

Sometimes, I need Times Square
 Midnight
On a mid-summer's Saturday
A million castaways... clashing
Amongst each other in waves of...
¡Punta!
¡Caraja!!
Me da! Me da!
Look @ the features
We all the same creatures
Same fake purses
Same old sneakers
Same old costumes
Different customs
All of us secretly searching
For substance
Fifty-Nine

in abundance
So, we search where the lights are always on
Now,
Brighter than what was ~~before~~
Once known of 40-Deuce
Used to be Pimps + Gangs
Now, it's Disney and Sporty coupes
You could once get shot on this block
Now, everywhere it's 40 Troops in blue
Pacing
Patiently waiting to mace...
or gag
Placed adjacent
To the brightest American flag
That America's ever had
Beyoncé poses for Pepsi
in Denim panties
What a clever ad...

Sixty

Hostess post next to her reads:
"The sweetest comeback in the history of ever"

The lights seem to stretch out forever
Our desperation stretches further
The lights so loud
You might see what you never heard of
Know there's a God somewhere
In this herd of... consumption
Maybe he's the naked cowboy
Flashing a grin. Sometimes
even God has to flash some skin
to get a rouse
The Israelites debate white devils
While an angel in lingerie
steals their crowd
Batman tries to get my attention...
Sixty-one

But his outfit didn't *WOW*
wasn't worth the
extra second of focus
 I allow.

My attention is devoured
by the neon culture that
towers aboves.
And to think,
I just came down here to be
showered in love.

Sixty-Two

City Love

In the middle of a block party
in Bed Stuy
Neighbors share slices
of the best pie
In East Buffalo,
Not far from the waterfall
A girl falls in love
Rapping the whole verse of Left Eye
Even when it's chilli like
Spring-time in the west side
Of Chicago
In a Juke Jam
In a Go-Go fest playing Backyard
Band in Largo
In the first taste of some Mambo Sauce
Or on a plate of
    Escargot
Sixty-Three

At a fancy place downtown
in D.C.
Riding down Georgia Ave
in seeing how things have changed
But you can still hear Chuck Brown
(on the slap!)
The guitar riff sweeter
than a Ravens touchdown...
on the Steelers...
in Pittsburgh...
During the playoffs
in the last seconds
A future memory made to become
a nostalgic past reference of
indigenous lost, and a
Hail to the Redskins
with a cornerstore beer
and a storefront church
      BLESSING.

Sixty-four

IN THE CREASE OF SOME SOUTH
OR NORTH SIDE STREETS
OF THE TRACKS LEFT QUESTIONED
IN FINDING GOD OUT IN THE EAST
OR IN THE BACK OF
A BEST WESTERN

ON THE CROSS-STREETS OF
| WESTERN | & | NORMANDIE |

IN THE RIOTS & IN THE CONFORMITY
IN INGLEWOOD WHERE 90° IS NORMAL HEAT

IN ALL THE PRAYERS
IN THE FORUM SEATS
IN THE BRACE AND EMBRACE OF
GANG-BANGING AS NORMALCY

Sixty-Five

In the taste of salt from the wind off the waves
of a torrent sea
In a conversation @ the Serving Spoon
over cheese grits
Morning Tea
In the Normal Sea of creatures
Creeping down the 405
In the tears and cries of the
neighborhoods gentrified
And the ones left fortified
In the core divide of the land
and
In the plans
of those that bought them up
In the Mom & Pop's
Turned Coffee Shops and
In the Row Homes left boarded
                                      Up!

Sixty-Six

IN THE LEAN OF ALL THE FIENDS
- AND -
IN ALL THE COKE LINES SNORTED UP
IN THE DISEASE OF ALL THE ARTERIES
IN THE MILD WINGS,
CRAB CAKES & CHEESE STEAKS
ORDERED UP!
IN THE ORDER OF
CHAOS

IN THE GRIND OF A 9-5
IN THE PEACE OF A DAY OFF...
IN THAT Peaceful TRADE OFF
IN ALL THE UNDERPAID AND
ALL THE ONES LAID OFF
IN THOSE WHO FIND THEMSELVES
IN THE HAVOC
IN ALL THE CONDOS & LOFTS
Sixty-Seven

IN ALL THOSE LOST IN THE LAVISH
IN THE PACE OF A PAPER-CHASER
IN THE HASTE OF A CRACK-ADDICT
IN THE WAYS BOTH ARE A CASE
OF THE SAME HABIT
IN THE MAGIC OF SPACE BETWEEN
TRIUMPH   AND   TRAGIC
IN THE BAR CRAWLS ON HUMP DAY OR
IN A LONG WALK ON THE SABBATH
IN THE PRACTICE OF EXCESS AND
IN THE PRIVELAGE OF ACCESS
IN THE RICH EVADING THE BRACKETS AND
IN THE POOR PAYING THE TAXES
IN THE BALANCE OF THAT AXIS

IN THE THIN LINE OF BLUE, AND

IN THE BLUES OF BLACKNESS
THE FACT IS... YOU MUST FIGHT THROUGH
THE MUD. THROUGH THE CRUD...
AND THE GRITTY. BUT IN SPITE OF IT ALL...
THERE IS LOVE IN THE CITY!
SIXTY-EIGHT

JEFTC

Just Enough For The City

ABOUT THE AUTHOR

Jo'rell H. Whitfield is an international spoken word artist, poet-playwright, and author. Born and reared in Queens, NY, Jo'rell's journey led him to study English at Morgan State University in Baltimore, MD. College provided the opportunity to hone in on his passion for performance poetry as well as written word; in 2008 he penned his first poetry book, "The Deferred Dream," and in 2014 released his first novel of the same title.

In 2008, he partnered with fellow writer and Morgan alum, Archie The Messenger, to create **Writing4MyLife**, a writing company that would also serve as the duo's stage name. He co-created the two-man spoken word play "No Stage," that featured at the *Syracuse Stage* in Syracuse, NY, the *Road Less Traveled* Theater in Buffalo, NY, and the *August Wilson Center* in Pittsburgh, PA.

As a performer, Jo'rell has been involved in the spoken word poetry scene for over 15 years, performing everywhere from open mic venues, to high schools, to colleges and universities in over 50 cities around the country. He has won countless poetry slams and has been featured in historical venues including The Nuyorican in New York, The Savoy in Los Angeles, and the Smithsonian in our Nation's capital. Jo'rell has also headlined at the annual Soothe Lounge in the Caribbean country of Antigua and Barbuda.

In addition to the spoken and written word, Jo'rell enjoys photography, is a true 'sneaker-head,' and loves to sing and dance to a vast variety of music. He is also the founder and lead website designer of **TriumphBeyondDesigns.com** – a design company geared to assist and boost businesses with their Internet Web-presence; and founder of **I Am Perspective** – a traveling 1-on-1 dialogue series aimed at creating a united society and genuine human connection through civilized conversations.

He is also a mixed-media artist – he designed the cover art for J.E.F.T.C.!

Follow Jo'rell on social media:

Instagram: @illestlyricist (The Author) | @thedeferreddream (The Series)
         @illestviews (The Photographer) | @triumphbeyonddesigns (Website Design)

Add To The City's Story

Just Enough For The City

Just Enough For The City

Just Enough For The City

Just Enough For The City

Just Enough For The City

Just Enough For The City

Just Enough For The City

Just Enough For The City

Just Enough For The City

Just Enough For The City

Just Enough For The City

Just Enough For The City

Just Enough For The City

Just Enough For The City

Just Enough For The City

Just Enough For The City

Just Enough For The City

Just Enough For The City

Just Enough For The City

Just Enough For The City

Just Enough For The City

Just Enough For The City

Just Enough For The City

Just Enough For The City

Just Enough For The City

Made in the USA
Middletown, DE
01 December 2024